PHILOCTETES

INCLUDING THE ILLUSTRATED ESSAY 'A NOTE ON THE HISTORY OF PHILOSOPHY'

by

SOPHOCLES

COMPASS CIRCLE

Philoctetes.
Written by Sophocles.
Translated by Richard Claverhouse Jebb.
Current edition published by Compass Circle in 2022.

Published by Compass Circle
Cover copyright ©2022 by Compass Circle.

Note:
All efforts have been made to preserve original spellings and punctuation of the original edition which may include old-fashioned English spellings of words and archaic variants.

This book is a product of its time and does not reflect the same views on race, gender, sexuality, ethnicity, and interpersonal relations as it would if it were written today.

For information contact :
information@compass-circle.com

Once in a lifetime
The longed-for tidal wave
Of justice can rise up,
And hope and history rhyme.

SOPHOCLES

SECRET WISDOM OF THE AGES SERIES

Life presents itself, it advances in a fast way. Life indeed never stops. It never stops until the end. The most diverse questions peek and fade in our minds. Sometimes we seek for answers. Sometimes we just let time go by.

The book you have now in your hands has been waiting to be discovered by you. This book may reveal the answers to some of your questions.

Books are friends. Friends who are always by your side and who can give you great ideas, advice or just comfort your soul.

A great book can make you see things in your soul that you have not yet discovered, make you see things in your soul that you were not aware of.

Great books can change your life for the better. They can make you understand fascinating theories, give you new ideas, inspire you to undertake new challenges or to walk along new paths.

Literature Classics like the one of *Philoctetes* are indeed a secret to many, but for those of us lucky enough to have discovered them, by one way or another, these books can enlighten us. They can open a wide range of possibilities to us. Because achieving greatness requires knowledge.

The series SECRET WISDOM OF THE AGES presented by Compass Circle try to bring you the great timeless masterpieces of literature, autobiographies and personal development,.

We welcome you to discover with us fascinating works by Nathaniel Hawthorne, Sir Arthur Conan Doyle, Edith Wharton, among others.

Contents

SOPHOCLES

Born   Sophocles
       497/496 BC
       Colonus, Attica

Died   406/405 BC
       Athens

SOPHOCLES

1

PHILOCTETES

PERSONS OF THE DRAMA.

Odysseus.

Neoptolemus.

Philoctetes.

Merchant (*a follower of Neoptolemus in disguise*).

Heracles.

Chorus of Sailors *belonging to the ship of Neoptolemus.*

SCENE: *On the north-east coast of Lemnos, near the promontory of Mount Hermaeum. A rocky cliff rises steeply from the sea-shore (cp. 1000 ff.): in it is seen the cave of Philoctetes.*

When Heracles was burned, by his own command, on Mount Oeta, the funeral-pile was kindled, at his prayer, by the youthful Philoctetes, son of Poeas, King of Malis. It was to Philoctetes that Heracles bequeathed the bow and arrows which he himself had received from Apollo.

Many years afterwards, Philoctetes came with seven ships to join the Greek armada which Agamemnon led against Troy. An oracle had enjoined that, in the course of their voyage, the Greeks should offer sacrifice to a deity named Chryse, whose altar was on a small island in the Aegean. Philoctetes alone knew where this altar was; he had once visited it in company with Heracles: and he guided the Greeks thither. The altar of Chryse stood in a sacred precinct under the open sky. As Philoctetes approached it, followed by the Greek chiefs, he was bitten in the foot by a serpent. His cries of pain made it impossible to perform the religious rites, which required the absence of all ill-omened sounds; and a noisome odour from the wound rendered the sufferer's presence a distress to his ship-mates. They conveyed him to the neighbouring coast of Lemnos; and there, at the bidding of the Atreidae, Odysseus put him ashore in his sleep, with only a scanty dole of food. The Greeks then sailed away to Troy. Lemnos was an uninhabited island. Philoctetes had his bow and arrows, and, though he could not crawl far from his cave, contrived to subsist by shooting birds.

Ten years had passed since the Greek chiefs did this inhuman deed. They were still besieging Troy. Achilles had fallen; Ajax had died by his own hand; and the Greeks were despondent. Their

5

prophet Calchas told them that, if they wished to learn the destiny of Ilium, they must consult a Trojan seer, Helenus, son of Priam. Helenus was made prisoner by a stratagem of Odysseus; and then declared that, before the Greeks could prevail, two things must be done. First, Philoctetes must be brought back from Lemnos: Troy could never fall, until the invincible arrows of Heracles were launched against its defenders. Secondly, Neoptolemus, the youthful son of Achilles, must come from the island of Scyros, and must receive his due heritage, the armour wrought for his father by the god Hephaestus; which, after that hero's death, had been awarded by the chiefs to Odysseus.

The Greeks obeyed these precepts. Phoenix and Odysseus went to Scyros, and brought the young Neoptolemus to Troy, where his father's armour was duly given to him. Odysseus then set out for Lemnos, accompanied by Neoptolemus,—each chief sailing in his own ship. At the moment when the play begins, they have just landed on the north-east coast of Lemnos.

PHILOCTETES.

ODYSSEUS.

THIS is the shore of the sea-girt land of Lemnos, untrodden of men and desolate. O thou whose sire was the noblest of the Greeks, true-bred son of Achilles, Neoptolemus,— here, long ago, I put ashore the Malian, the son of Poeas, (having charge from my chiefs so to do,)—his foot all ulcerous with a gnawing sore,—when neither drink-offering nor sacrifice could be attempted by us in peace, but with his fierce, ill-omened cries he filled the whole camp continually, shrieking, moaning. But what need to speak of that? 'Tis no time for many words, lest he learn that I am here, and I waste the whole plan whereby I think to take him anon.

Come, to work!—'tis for thee to help in what remains, and to seek where in this region is a cave with twofold mouth, such that in cold weather either front offers a sunny seat, but in summer a breeze wafts sleep through the tunnelled grot. And a little below, on the left hand, perchance thou wilt see a spring, if it hath not failed.

Move thither silently, and signify to me whether he still dwells in this same place, or is to be sought elsewhere,—that so our further course may be explained by me, and heard by thee, and sped by the joint work of both.

NEOPTOLEMUS.

King Odysseus, the task that thou settest lies not far off;
methinks I see such a cave as thou hast described.

OD. Above thee, or below? I perceive it not.

NE. Here, high up;—and of footsteps not a sound.

OD. Look that he be not lodged there, asleep.

NE. I see an empty chamber,—no man therein.

OD. And no provision in it for man's abode?

NE. Aye, a mattress of leaves, as if for some one who
makes his lodging here.

OD. And all else is bare? Nought else beneath the roof?

NE. Just a rude cup of wood, the work of a sorry crafts-
man; and this tinder-stuff therewith.

OD. His is the household store whereof thou tellest.

NE. Ha! Yes, and here are some rags withal, drying in
the sun,—stained with matter from some grievous sore.

OD. The man dwells in these regions, clearly, and is
somewhere not far off; how could one go far afield, with
foot maimed by that inveterate plague? No, he hath gone
forth in quest of food, or of some soothing herb, haply, that
he hath noted somewhere. Send thine attendant, therefore,
to keep watch, lest the foe come on me unawares; for he
would rather take me than all the Greeks beside.

NE. Enough, the man is going, and the path shall be
watched.—And now, if thou wouldst say more, proceed.

[*Exit* Attendant, *on the spectators' left.*

OD. Son of Achilles, thou must be loyal to thy mission,—and not with thy body alone. Shouldst thou hear some new thing, some plan unknown to thee till now, thou must help it; for to help is thy part here.

NE. What is thy bidding?

OD. Thou must beguile the mind of Philoctetes by a story told in thy converse with him. When he asks thee who and whence thou art, say, the son of Achilles,—there must be no deception touching that; but thou art homeward bound,—thou hast left the fleet of the Achaean warriors, and hast conceived a deadly hatred for them; who, when they had moved thee by their prayers to come from home, deemed thee not worthy of the arms of Achilles,—deigned not to give them to thee when thou camest and didst claim them by right,—but made them over to Odysseus. Of me, say what thou wilt,—the vilest of vile reproaches;—thou wilt cost me no pang by that;—but if thou fail to do this deed, thou wilt bring sorrow on all our host. For if yon man's bow is not to be taken, never canst thou sack the realm of Dardanus.

And mark why thine intercourse with him may be free from mistrust or danger, while mine cannot. *Thou* hast come to Troy under no oath to any man, and by no constraint; nor hadst thou part in the earlier voyage: but none of these things can I deny. And so, if he shall perceive me

9

while he is still master of his bow, I am lost, and thou, as my comrade, wilt share my doom. No; the thing that must be plotted is just this,—how thou mayest win the resistless arms by stealth. I well know, my son, that by nature thou art not apt to utter or contrive such guile; yet, seeing that victory is a sweet prize to gain, bend thy will thereto; our honesty shall be shown forth another time. But now lend thyself to me for one little knavish day, and then, through all thy days to come, be called the most righteous of mankind.

NE. When counsels pain my ear, son of Laertes, then I abhor to aid them with my hand. It is not in my nature to compass aught by evil arts,—nor was it, as men say, in my sire's. But I am ready to take the man by force,—not by fraud;—for, having the use of one foot only, he cannot prevail in fight against us who are so many. And yet, having been sent to act with thee, I am loth to be called traitor. But my wish, O King, is to do right and miss my aim, rather than succeed by evil ways.

OD. Son of brave sire, time was when I too, in my youth, had a slow tongue and a ready hand: but now, when I come forth to the proof, I see that words, not deeds, are ever the masters among men.

NE. What, then, is thy command? What, but that I should lie?

OD. I say that thou art to take Philoctetes by guile.

NE. And why by guile rather than by persuasion?

OD. He will never listen; and by force thou canst not take him.

NE. Hath he such dread strength to make him bold?

OD. Shafts inevitable, and winged with death.

NE. None may dare, then, e'en to approach that foe?

OD. No, unless thou take him by guile, as I say.

NE. Thou thinkest it no shame, then, to speak falsehoods?

OD. No, if the falsehood brings deliverance.

NE. And how shall one have the face to speak those words?

OD. When thy deed promises gain, 'tis unmeet to shrink.

NE. And what gain is it for me, that he should come to Troy?

OD. With these shafts alone can Troy be taken.

NE. Then *I* am not to be the conqueror, as ye said?

OD. Neither thou apart from these, nor these from thee.

NE. 'Twould seem that we must try to win them, if it stands thus.

OD. Know that, if thou dost this thing, two prizes are thine.

NE. What are they? Tell me, and I will not refuse the deed.

OD. Thou wilt be called at once wise and valiant.

NE. Come what may, I'll do it, and cast off all shame.

OD. Art thou mindful, then, of the counsels that I gave?

NE. Be sure of it,—now that once I have consented.

OD. Do thou, then, stay here, in wait for him; but I will go away, lest I be espied with thee, and will send our watcher back to the ship. And, if ye seem to be tarrying at all beyond the due time, I will send that same man hither again, disguised as the captain of a merchant-ship, that secrecy may aid us; and then, my son, as he tells his artful story, take such hints as may help thee from the tenor of his words.

Now I will go to the ship, having left this charge with thee; and may speeding Hermes, the lord of stratagem, lead us on, and Victory, even Athena Polias, who saves me ever!

[*Exit* Odysseus, *on the spectators' left.*

CHORUS.

A stranger in a strange land, what am I to hide, what am I to speak, O Master, before a man who will be swift to think evil? Be thou my guide: his skill excels all other skill, his counsel hath no peer, with whom is the sway of the godlike sceptre given by Zeus. And to thee, my son, that sovereign power hath descended from of old; tell me, therefore, wherein I am to serve thee.

NE. For the present,—as haply thou wouldst behold the place where he abides on ocean's verge, survey it fearlessly: but when the dread wayfarer, who hath left this dwelling, shall return, come forward at my beck from time to time, and try to help as the moment may require.

CH. Long have I been careful of that care, my prince,—that mine eye should be watchful for thy good, before all else. And now tell me, in what manner of shelter hath he made his abode? In what region is he? 'Twere not unseasonable for me to learn, lest he surprise me from some quarter. What is the place of his wandering, or of his rest? Where planteth he his steps, within his dwelling, or abroad?

NE. Here thou seest his home, with its two portals,—his rocky cell.

CH. And its hapless inmate,—whither is he gone?

NE. I doubt not but he is trailing his painful steps somewhere near this spot, in quest of food. For rumour saith that in this fashion he lives, seeking prey with his winged shafts, all-wretched that he is; and no healer of his woe draws nigh unto him.

CH. I pity him, to think how, with no man to care for him, and seeing no companion's face, suffering, lonely evermore, he is vexed by fierce disease, and bewildered by each want as it arises. How, how doth he endure in his misery? Alas, the dark dealings of the gods! Alas, hapless races of men, whose destiny exceeds due measure!

This man,—noble, perchance, as any scion of the noblest house,—reft of all life's gifts, lies lonely, apart from his fellows, with the dappled or shaggy beasts of the field, piteous alike in his torments and his hunger, bearing anguish that finds no cure; while the mountain nymph, babbling Echo,

13

appearing afar, makes answer to his bitter cries.

NE. Nought of this is a marvel to me. By heavenly ordinance, if such as I may judge, those first sufferings came on him from relentless Chrysè; and the woes that now he bears, with none to tend him, surely he bears by the providence of some god, that so he should not bend against Troy the resistless shafts divine, till the time be fulfilled when, as men say, Troy is fated by those shafts to fall.

CH. Hush, peace, my son! NE. What now? CH. a sound rose on the air, such as might haunt the lips of a man in weary pain.—From this point it came, I think,—or this.—It smites, it smites indeed upon my ear—the voice of one who creeps painfully on his way; I cannot mistake that grievous cry of human anguish from afar,—its accents are too clear.

Then turn thee, O my son— NE. Say, whither?— CH. —to new counsels: for the man is not far off, but near; not with music of the reed he cometh, like shepherd in the pastures,—no, but with far-sounding moan, as he stumbles, perchance, from stress of pain, or as he gazes on the haven that hath no ship for guest: loud is his cry, and dread.

ENTER PHILOCTETES, *ON THE SPECTATORS' RIGHT.*

PH. O strangers!
Who may ye be, and from what country have ye put into this land, that is harbourless and desolate? What should I deem to be your city or your race?
The fashion of your garb is Greek,—most welcome to

14

my sight,—but I fain would hear your speech: and do not shrink from me in fear, or be scared by my wild looks; nay, in pity for one so wretched and so lonely, for a sufferer so desolate and so friendless, speak to me, if indeed ye have come as friends.—Oh, answer! 'Tis not meet that I should fail of this, at least, from you, or ye from me.

NE. Then know this first, good Sir, that we are Greeks,—since thou art fain to learn that.

PH. O well-loved sound! Ah, that I should indeed be greeted by such a man, after so long a time! What quest, my son, hath drawn thee towards these shores, and to this spot? What enterprise? What kindliest of winds? Speak, tell me all, that I may know who thou art.

NE. My birthplace is the seagirt Scyros; I am sailing homeward; Achilles was my sire; my name is Neoptolemus: —thou know'st all.

PH. O son of well-loved father and dear land, foster-child of aged Lycomedes, on what errand hast thou touched this coast? Whence art thou sailing?

NE. Well, it is from Ilium that I hold my present course.

PH. What? Thou wast not, certainly, our shipmate at the beginning of the voyage to Ilium.

NE. Hadst thou, indeed, a part in that emprise?

PH. O my son, then thou know'st not who is before thee?

NE. How should I know one whom I have never seen before?

PH. Then thou hast not even heard my name, or any rumour of those miseries by which I was perishing?

NE. Be assured that I know nothing of what thou askest.

PH. O wretched indeed that I am, O abhorred of heaven, that no word of this my plight should have won its way to my home, or to any home of Greeks! No, the men who wickedly cast me out keep their secret and laugh, while my plague still rejoices in its strength, and grows to more!

O my son, O boy whose father was Achilles, behold, I am he of whom haply thou hast heard as lord of the bow of Heracles,—I am the son of Poeas, Philoctetes, whom the two chieftains and the Cephallenian king foully cast upon this solitude, when I was wasting with a fierce disease, stricken down by the furious bite of the destroying serpent; with that plague for sole companion, O my son, those men put me out here, and were gone,—when from sea-girt Chrysè they touched at this coast with their fleet. Glad, then, when they saw me asleep—after much tossing on the waves—in the shelter of a cave upon the shore, they abandoned me,—first putting out a few rags,—good enough for such a wretch,— and a scanty dole of food withal:—may Heaven give them the like!

Think now, my son, think what a waking was mine, when they had gone, and I rose from sleep that day! What bitter tears started from mine eyes,—what miseries were those that I bewailed when I saw that the ships with which I had sailed were all gone, and that there was no man in the place,—not one to help, not one to ease the burden of the sickness that vexed me,—when, looking all around, I could find no provision, save for anguish—but of that a plenteous store, my son!

So time went on for me, season by season; and, alone in this narrow house, I was fain to meet each want by mine own service. For hunger's needs this bow provided, bringing down the winged doves; and, whatever my string-sped shaft might strike, I, hapless one, would crawl to it myself, trailing my wretched foot just so far; or if, again, water had to be fetched,—or if (when the frost was out, perchance, as oft in winter) a bit of fire-wood had to be broken,—I would creep forth, poor wretch, and manage it. Then fire would be lacking; but by rubbing stone on stone I would at last draw forth the hidden spark; and this it is that keeps life in me from day to day. Indeed, a roof over my head, and fire therewith, gives all that I want—save release from my disease.

Come now, my son, thou must learn what manner of isle this is. No mariner approaches it by choice; there is no anchorage; there is no sea-port where he can find a gainful market or a kindly welcome. This is not a place to which prudent men make voyages. Well, suppose that some one has put in against his will; such things may oft happen in the long course of a man's life. These visitors, when they come, have compassionate words for me; and perchance, moved by pity, they give me a little food, or some raiment: but there is one thing that no one will do, when I speak of it,—take me safe home; no, this is now the tenth year that I am wearing out my wretched days, in hunger and in misery, feeding the plague that is never sated with my flesh.

Thus have the Atreidae and the proud Odysseus dealt with me, my son: may the Olympian gods some day give them the like sufferings, in requital for mine!

CH. Methinks I too pity thee, son of Poeas, in like measure with thy former visitors.

NE. And I am myself a witness to thy words,—I know that they are true; for I have felt the villainy of the Atreidae and the proud Odysseus.

PH. What, hast thou, too, a grief against the accursed sons of Atreus,—a cause to resent ill-usage?

NE. Oh that it might be mine one day to wreak my hatred with my hand, that so Mycenae might learn, and Sparta, that Scyros also is a mother of brave men!

PH. Well said, my son! Now wherefore hast thou come in this fierce wrath which thou denouncest against them?

NE. Son of Poeas, I will speak out—and yet 'tis hard to speak—concerning the outrage that I suffered from them at my coming. When fate decreed that Achilles should die—

PH. Ah me! Tell me no more, until I first know this— say'st thou that the son of Peleus is dead?

NE. Dead,—by no mortal hand, but by a god's; laid low, as men say, by the arrow of Phoebus.

PH. Well, noble alike are the slayer and the slain! I scarce know, my son, which I should do first,—inquire into thy wrong, or mourn the dead.

NE. Methinks thine own sorrows, unhappy man, are enough for thee, without mourning for the woes of thy neighbour.

PH. Thou sayest truly.—Resume thy story, then, and tell me wherein they did thee a despite.

NE. They came for me in a ship with gaily decked prow,—princely Odysseus, and he who watched over my father's youth,—saying, (whether truly or falsely, I know not,) that since my father had perished, fate now forbad that the towers of Troy should be taken by any hand but mine.

Saying that these things stood thus, my friend, they made me pause not long ere I set forth in haste,—chiefly through my yearning towards the dead, that I might see him before burial,—for I had never seen him; then, besides, there was a charm in their promise, if, when I went, I should sack the towers of Troy.

It was now the second day of my voyage, when, sped by breeze and oar, I drew nigh to cruel Sigeum. And when I landed, straightway all the host thronged around me with greetings, vowing that they saw their lost Achilles once more alive.

He, then, lay dead; and I, hapless one, when I had wept for him, presently went to the Atreidae,—to friends, as I well might deem,—and claimed my father's arms, with all else that had been his. O, 'twas a shameless answer that they made! 'Seed of Achilles, thou canst take all else that was thy sire's; but of those arms another man now is lord,—the son of Laertes.' The tears came into my eyes,—I sprang up in passionate anger, and said in my bitterness,—'Wretch! What, have ye dared to give my arms to another man, without my leave?' Then said Odysseus,—for he chanced to be near,—'Yea, boy, this award of theirs is just; I saved the arms and their master at his need.' Then straightway, in my fury, I began to hurl all manner of taunts at him, and spared not one, if I was indeed to be robbed of my arms by *him.* At this point,—stung by the abuse, though not prone to wrath,—he answered,—'Thou wast not here with us, but absent from thy duty. And since thou must talk so saucily, thou shalt never carry those arms back to Scyros.'

Thus upbraided, thus insulted, I sail for home, despoiled of mine own by that worst offspring of an evil breed, Odysseus. And yet he, I think, is less to blame than the rulers. For an army, like a city, hangs wholly on its leaders; and when men do lawless deeds, 'tis the counsel of their teachers that corrupts them. My tale is told; and may the foe of the Atreidae have the favour of Heaven, as he hath mine!

CH. Goddess of the hills, all-fostering Earth, mother of Zeus most high, thou through whose realm the great Pactolus rolls golden sands,—there also, dread Mother, I called upon thy name, when all the insults of the Atreidae were being heaped upon this man,—when they were giving his sire's armour, that peerless marvel, to the son of Lartius—hear it, thou immortal one, who ridest on bull-slaughtering lions!

PH. It seems that ye have come to me, friends, well commended by a common grief; and your story is of a like strain with mine, so that I can recognise the work of the Atreidae and of Odysseus. For well I know that he would lend his tongue to any base pretext, to any villainy, if thereby he could hope to compass some dishonest end. No, 'tis not at this that I wonder, but rather that the elder Ajax, if he was there, could endure to see it.

NE. Ah, friend, he was no more; I should never have been thus plundered while he lived.

PH. How sayest thou? What, is he, too, dead and gone?

NE. Think of him as of one who sees the light no more.

PH. Woe is me! But the son of Tydeus, and the offspring of Sisyphus that was bought by Laertes—they will not die; for they ought not to live.

NE. Not they, be sure of it; no, they are now prospering full greatly in the Argive host.

PH. And what of my brave old friend, Nestor of Pylos,—

is he not alive? *Their* mischiefs were often baffled by his wise counsels.

NE. Aye, he has trouble now; death has taken Antilochus, the son that was at his side.

PH. Ah me! These two, again, whom thou hast named, are men of whose death I had least wished to hear. Alas! What are we to look for, when these have died, and, here again, Odysseus lives,—when he, in their place, should have been numbered with the dead?

NE. A clever wrestler he; but even clever schemes, Philoctetes, are often tripped up.

PH. Now tell me, I pray thee, where was Patroclus in this thy need,—he whom thy father loved so well?

NE. He, too, was dead. And to be brief, I would tell thee this,—war takes no evil man by choice, but good men always.

PH. I bear thee witness;—and for that same reason I will ask thee how fares a man of little worth, but shrewd of tongue and clever—

NE. Surely this will be no one but Odysseus?—

PH. I meant not him:—but there was one Thersites, who could never be content with brief speech, though all men chafed:—know'st thou if he is alive?

NE. I saw him not, but heard that he still lives.

PH. It was his due. No evil thing has been known to perish; no, the gods take tender care of such, and have a strange joy in turning back from Hades all things villainous and knavish, while they are ever sending the just and the good out of life. How am I to deem of these things, or wherein shall I praise them, when, praising the ways of the gods, I find that the gods are evil?

NE. Son of Oetean sire, I, at least, shall be on my guard henceforth against Ilium and the Atreidae, nor look on them save from afar; and where the worse man is stronger than the good,—where honesty fails and the dastard bears sway,—among such men will I never make my friends. No, rocky Scyros shall suffice for me henceforth, nor shall I ask a better home.

Now to my ship! And thou, son of Poeas, farewell,—heartily farewell; and the gods deliver thee from thy sickness, even as thou wouldst! But we must be going, so that we may set forth whenever the god permits our voyage.

PH. Do ye start now, my son?

NE. Aye, prudence bids us watch the weather near our ship, rather than from afar.

PH. Now by thy father and by thy mother, my son —by all that is dear to thee in thy home—solemnly I implore thee, leave me not thus forlorn, helpless amid these miseries in which I live,—such as thou seest, and many as thou hast heard! Nay, spare a passing thought to me.—Great is the discomfort, I well know, of such a freight ;—yet bear with it: to noble minds baseness is hateful, and a good deed is glorious. Forsake this task, and thy fair name is sullied; perform it, my son, and a rich meed of glory will be thine, if I return alive to Oeta's land. Come, the trouble lasts not one whole day:—make the effort—take and thrust me where thou wilt, in hold, in prow, in stern,—wherever I shall least annoy my ship-mates.

O consent, by the great Zeus of suppliants, my son,—be persuaded! I supplicate thee on my knees, infirm as I am, poor wretch, and maimed! Nay, leave me not thus desolate, far from the steps of men! Nay, bring me safely to thine own home, or to Euboea, Chalcodon's seat; and thence it will be no long journey for me to Oeta, and the Trachinian heights, and the fair-flowing Spercheius, that thou mayest show me to my beloved sire; of whom I have long feared that he may have gone from me. For often did I summon him by those who came, with imploring prayers that he would himself send a ship, and fetch me home. But either he is dead, or else, methinks, my messengers—as was likely—made small account of my concerns, and hastened on their homeward voyage.

Now, however—since in thee I have found one who can carry at once my message and myself—do thou save me, do thou show me mercy,—seeing how all human destiny is full of the fear and the peril that good fortune may be followed by evil. He who stands clear of trouble should beware of dangers; and when a man lives at ease, then it is that he should look most closely to his life, lest ruin come on it by stealth.

Ch. Have pity, O king; he hath told of a struggle with sufferings manifold and grievous; may the like befall no friend of mine! And if, my prince, thou hatest the hateful Atreidae, then, turning their misdeed to this man's gain, I would waft him in thy good swift ship to the home for which he yearns, that so thou flee the just wrath of Heaven.

Ne. Beware lest, though now, as a spectator, thou art pliant, yet, when wearied of his malady by consorting with it, thou be found no longer constant to these words.

Ch. No, verily: never shalt thou have cause to utter that reproach against me!

Ne. Nay, then, it were shame that the stranger should find me less prompt than thou art to serve him at his need.—Come, if it please you, let us sail: let the man set forth at once; our ship, for her part, will carry him, and will not refuse.—Only may the gods convey us safely out of this land, and hence to our haven, wheresoever it be!

Ph. O most joyful day! O kindest friend—and ye, good sailors—would that I could prove to you in deeds what love ye have won from me! Let us be going, my son, when thou and I have made a solemn farewell to the homeless home within,—that thou mayest e'en learn by what means I sustained life, and how stout a heart hath been mine. For I believe that the bare sight would have deterred any other man from enduring such a lot; but I have been slowly schooled by necessity to patience.

[*Neoptolemus is about to follow Philoctetes into the cave.*

CH. Stay, let us give heed:—two men are coming, one a seaman of thy ship, the other a stranger: ye should hear their tidings before ye go in.

ENTER MERCHANT, *ON THE SPECTATORS' LEFT, ACCOMPANIED BY A*
SAILOR.

ME. Son of Achilles, I asked my companion here,—who, with two others, was guarding thy ship,—to tell me where thou mightest be,—since I have fallen in with thee, when I did not expect it, by the chance of coming to anchor off the same coast. Sailing, in trader's wise, with no great company, homeward bound from Ilium to Peparethus with its cluster-laden vines,—when I heard that the sailors were all of thy crew, I resolved not to go on my voyage in silence, without first giving thee my news, and reaping guerdon due. Thou knowest nothing, I suspect, of thine own affairs— the new designs that the Greeks have regarding thee,—nay, not designs merely, but deeds in progress, and no longer tarrying.

NE. Truly, Sir, the grace shown me by thy forethought, if I be not unworthy, shall live in my grateful thoughts. But tell me just what it is whereof thou hast spoken,—that I may learn what strange design on the part of the Greeks thou announcest to me.

ME. Pursuers have started in quest of thee with ships,— the aged Phoenix and the sons of Theseus.

NE. To bring me back by force, or by fair words?

ME. I know not; but I have come to tell thee what I have heard.

NE. Can Phoenix and his comrades be showing such zeal on such an errand, to please the Atreidae?

ME. The errand is being done, I can assure thee,—and without delay.

NE. Why, then, was not Odysseus ready to sail for this purpose, and to bring the message himself? Or did some fear restrain him?

ME. Oh, he and the son of Tydeus were setting forth in pursuit of another man, as I was leaving port.

NE. Who was this other in quest of whom Odysseus himself was sailing?

ME. There was a man… But tell me first who that is yonder,—and whatever thou sayest, speak not loud.

NE. Sir, thou seest the renowned Philoctetes.

ME. Ask me no more, then, but convey thyself with all speed out of this land.

PH. What is he saying, my son? Why is the sailor trafficking with thee about me in these dark whispers?

NE. I know not his meaning yet; but whatever he would

say he must say openly to thee and me and these.

ME. Seed of Achilles, do not accuse me to the army of saying what I should not; I receive many benefits from them for my services,—as a poor man may.

NE. I am the foe of the Atreidae, and this man is my best friend, because he hates them. Since, then, thou hast come with a kindly purpose towards me, thou must not keep from us any part of the tidings that thou hast heard.

ME. See what thou doest, my son.

NE. I am well aware.

ME. I will hold thee accountable.

NE. Do so, but speak.

ME. I obey. 'Tis in quest of this man that those two are sailing whom I named to thee,—the son of Tydeus and mighty Odysseus,—sworn to bring him, either by winning words or by constraining force. And all the Achaeans heard this plainly from Odysseus,—for his confidence of success was higher than his comrade's.

NE. And wherefore, after so long a time, did the Atreidae turn their thoughts towards this man, whom long since they had cast forth? What was the yearning that came to them,—what compulsion, or what vengeance, from gods who requite evil deeds?

ME. I can expound all that to thee,—since it seems that thou hast not heard it. There was a seer of noble birth, a son of Priam,—by name Helenus; whom this man, going forth by night,—this guileful Odysseus, of whom all shameful and dishonouring words are spoken,—made his prisoner; and, leading him in bonds, showed him publicly to the Achaeans, a goodly prize: who then prophesied to them whatso else they asked, and that they should never sack the towers of Troy, unless by winning words they should bring this man from the island whereon he now dwells.

And the son of Laertes, when he heard the seer speak thus, straightway promised that he would bring this man and show him to the Achaeans,—most likely, he thought, as a willing captive,—but, if reluctant, then by force; adding that, should he fail in this, whoso wished might have his head.—Thou hast heard all, my son, and I commend speed to thee, and to any man for whom thou carest.

PH. Hapless that I am! Hath he, that utter pest, sworn to bring me by persuasion to the Achaeans? As soon shall I be persuaded, when I am dead, to come up from Hades to the light, as his father came!

ME. I know nothing about that:—but I must go to ship, and may Heaven be with you both for all good.

[*Exit* Merchant.

PH. Now is not this wondrous, my son, that the offspring of Laertes should have hoped, by means of soft words, to lead me forth from his ship and show me amidst the Greeks? No! sooner would I hearken to that deadliest of my foes, the viper which made me the cripple that I am! But there is nothing that *he* would not say, or dare; and now I know that he will be here. Come, my son, let us be moving, that a wide sea may part us from the ship of Odysseus. Let us go: good speed in good season brings sleep and rest, when toil is o'er.

NE. We will sail, then, as soon as the head-wind falls; at present it is adverse.

PH. 'Tis ever fair sailing, when thou fleest from evil.

NE. Nay, but this weather is against them also.

PH. No wind comes amiss to pirates, when there is a chance to steal, or to rob by force.

NE. Well, let us be going, if thou wilt,—when thou hast taken from within whatever thou needest or desirest most.

PH. Aye, there are some things that I need,—though the choice is not large.

NE. What is there that will not be found on board my ship?

PH. I keep by me a certain herb, wherewith I can always best assuage this wound, till it is wholly soothed.

NE. Fetch it, then. Now, what else wouldst thou take?

PH. Any of these arrows that may have been forgotten, and may have slipped away from me,—lest I leave it to be another's prize.

NE. Is that indeed the famous bow which thou art holding?

PH. This, and no other, that I carry in my hand.

NE. Is it lawful for me to have a nearer view of it,—to handle it and to salute it as a god?

PH. To thee, my son, this shall be granted, and anything else in my power that is for thy good.

NE. I certainly long to touch it,—but my longing is on this wise;—if it be lawful, I should be glad; if not, think no more of it.

PH. Thy words are reverent, and thy wish, my son, is lawful; for thou alone hast given to mine eyes the light of life,—the hope to see the Oetean land,—to see mine aged father and my friends,—thou who, when I lay beneath the feet of my foes, hast lifted me beyond their reach. Be of good cheer; the bow shall be thine, to handle, and to return to the hand that gave it; thou shalt be able to vaunt that, in reward of thy kindness, thou, alone of mortals, hast touched it; for 'twas by a good deed that I myself won it.

NE. I rejoice to have found thee, and to have gained thy friendship; for whosoever knows how to render benefit for benefit must prove a friend above price.—Go in, I pray thee.

PH. Yes, and I will lead thee in; for my sick estate craves the comfort of thy presence. [*They enter the cave.*

CH. I have heard in story, but seen not with mine eyes, how he who once came near the bed of Zeus was bound upon a swift wheel by the almighty son of Cronus; but of no other mortal know I, by hearsay or by sight, that hath encountered a doom so dreadful as this man's; who, though he had wronged none by force or fraud, but lived at peace with his fellow-men, was left to perish thus cruelly.

Verily I marvel how, as he listened in his solitude to the surges that beat around him, he kept his hold upon a life so full of woe; where he was neighbour to himself alone,—powerless to walk,—with no one in the land to be near him while he suffered, in whose ear he could pour forth the lament, awaking response, for the plague that gnawed his flesh and drained his blood;—no one to assuage the burning flux, oozing from the ulcers of his envenomed foot, with healing herbs gathered from the bounteous earth, so often as the torment came upon him.

Then would he creep this way or that, with painful steps, like a child without kindly nurse, to any place whence his need might be supplied, whenever the devouring anguish abated; gathering not for food the fruit of holy Earth, nor aught else that we mortals gain by toil; save when haply he found wherewith to stay his hunger by winged shafts from his swift-smiting bow. Ah, joyless was his life, who for ten years never knew the gladness of the wine-cup, but still bent his way towards any stagnant pool that he could descry as he gazed around him.

But now, after those troubles, he shall be happy and mighty at the last; for he hath met with the son of a noble race, who in the fulness of many months bears him on sea-cleaving ship to his home, haunt of Malian nymphs, and to the banks of the Spercheius; where, above Oeta's heights, the lord of the brazen shield drew near to the gods, amid the splendour of the lightnings of his sire.

NE. I pray thee, come on. Why art thou so silent? Why dost thou halt, as if dismayed, without a cause?

PH. Alas, alas!

NE. What is the matter? PH. Nothing serious:—go on, my son.

NE. Art thou in pain from the disease that vexes thee?

PH. No indeed,—no, I think I am better just now.—Ye gods!

NE. Why groanest thou thus, and callest on the gods?

PH. That they may come to us with power to save and soothe.—Ah me!—ah me!

NE. What ails thee? Speak,—persist not in this silence:— 'tis plain that something is amiss with thee.

PH. I am lost, my son—I can never hide my trouble from you:—ah, it pierces me, it pierces! O misery,—O wretched that I am! I am undone, my son—it devours me.—Oh, for the gods' love, if thou hast a sword ready to thy hand, strike at my heel,—shear it off straightway—heed not my life! Quick, quick, my son!

NE. And what new thing hath come on thee so suddenly, that thou bewailest thyself with such loud laments?

PH. Thou knowest, my son. NE. What is it? PH. Thou

knowest, boy. NE. What is the matter with thee? I know not PH. How canst thou help knowing? Oh, oh!

NE. Dread, indeed, is the burden of the malady.

PH. Aye, dread beyond telling. Oh, pity me!

NE. What shall I do? PH. Forsake me not in fear. This visitant comes but now and then,—when she hath been sated, haply, with her roamings.

NE. Ah, hapless one! Hapless, indeed, art thou found in all manner of woe! Shall I take hold of thee, or lend thee a helping hand?

PH. No, no:—but take this bow of mine, I pray thee,—as thou didst ask of me just now,—and keep it safe till this present access of my disease is past. For indeed sleep falls on me when this plague is passing away, nor can the pain cease sooner; but ye must allow me to slumber in peace. And if meanwhile those men come, I charge thee by Heaven that in no wise, willingly or unwillingly, thou give up this bow to them,—lest thou bring destruction at once on thyself and on me, who am thy suppliant.

NE. Have no fears as to my caution. The bow shall pass into no hands but thine and mine.—Give it to me, and may good luck come with it!

PH. There it is, my son:—and pray the jealous gods that it may not bring thee troubles, such as it brought to me and to him who was its lord before me.

NE. Ye gods, grant this to us twain! Grant us a voyage

prosperous and swift, whithersoever the god approves and our purpose tends!

PH. Nay, my son, I fear that thy prayers are vain; for lo, once more the dark blood oozes drop by drop from the depths, and I look for worse to come. Ah me, oh, oh! Thou hapless foot, what torment wilt thou work for me! It creeps on me,—it is drawing near! Woe, woe is me! Ye know it now:—flee not, I pray you!

O Cephallenian friend, would that this anguish might cleave to thee, and transfix thy breast! Ah me! Ah me! O ye chieftains twain, Agamemnon, Menelaus, would that ye, instead of me, might have this malady upon you, and for as long! Ah me, ah me! O Death, Death, when I am thus ever calling thee, day by day, why canst thou never come? O my son, generous youth, come, seize me, burn me up, true-hearted friend, in yonder fire, famed as Lemnian:—I, too, once deemed it lawful to do the same unto the son of Zeus, for the meed of these same arms, which are now in thy keeping. What sayest thou, boy,—what sayest thou? Why art thou silent? Where are thy thoughts, my son?

NE. I have long been grieving in my heart for thy load of pain.

PH. Nay, my son, have good hope withal; this visitor comes sharply, but goes quickly. Only, I beseech thee, leave me not alone.

NE. Fear not, we will remain. PH. Thou wilt remain?

NE. Be sure of it.

PH. Well, I do not ask to put thee on thine oath, my son

NE. Rest satisfied: 'tis not lawful for me to go without thee.

PH. Thy hand for pledge! NE. I give it—to stay.

PH. Now take me yonder, yonder— NE. Whither meanest thou? PH. Up yonder—

NE. What is this new frenzy? Why gazest thou on the vault above us?

PH. Let me go, let me go! NE. Whither? PH. Let me go I say!

NE. I will not. PH. Thou wilt kill me, if thou touch me.

NE. There, then—I release thee, since thou art calmer.

PH. O Earth, receive me as I die, here and now! This pain no longer suffers me to stand upright.

NE. Methinks sleep will come to him ere long: see, his head sinks backward; yes, a sweat is bathing his whole body and a thin stream of dark blood hath broken forth from his heel.

Come, friends, let us leave him in quietness, that he may fall on slumber.

CH. Sleep, stranger to anguish, painless Sleep, come, at our prayer, with gentle breath, come with benison, O king and keep before his eyes such light as is spread before them now; come, I pray thee, come with power to heal!

O son, bethink thee where thou wilt stand, and to what

counsels thou wilt next turn our course. Thou seest how 'tis now! Why should we delay to act? Opportunity, arbiter of all action, oft wins a great victory by one swift stroke.

NE. Nay, though he hears nothing, I see that in vain have we made this bow our prize, if we sail without him. His must be the crown; 'tis he that the god bade us bring. 'Twere a foul shame for us to boast of deeds in which failure hath waited on fraud.

CH. Nay, my son, the god will look to that. But when thou answerest me again, softly, softly whisper thy words, my son: for sick men's restless sleep is ever quick of vision.

But, I pray thee, use thine utmost care to win that prize, that great prize, by stealth. For if thou maintain thy present purpose towards this man,—thou knowest of what purpose I speak,—a prudent mind can foresee troubles most grievous.

Now, my son, now the wind is fair for thee:—sightless and helpless, the man lies stretched in darkness,—sleep in the heat is sound,—with no command of hand or foot, but reft of all his powers, like unto one who rests with Hades.

Take heed, look if thy counsels be seasonable: so far as my thoughts can seize the truth, my son, the best strategy is that which gives no alarm.

NE. Hush, I say, and let not your wits forsake you:—yon man opens his eyes, and lifts his head.

PH. Ah, sunlight following on sleep,—ah, ye friendly

watchers, undreamed of by my hopes! Never, my son, could I have dared to look for this,—that thou shouldest have patience to wait so tenderly upon my sufferings, staying beside me, and helping to relieve me. The Atreidae, certainly, those valiant chieftains, had no heart to bear this burden so lightly. But thy nature, my son, is noble, and of noble breed; and so thou hast made little of all this, though loud cries and noisome odours vexed thy senses.

And now, since the plague seems to allow me a space of forgetfulness and peace at last, raise me thyself, my son, set me on my feet, so that, when the faintness shall at length release me, we may set forth to the ship, and delay not to sail.

Ne. Right glad am I to see thee, beyond my hope, living and breathing, free from pain; for, judged by the sufferings that afflict thee, thy symptoms seemed to speak of death.— But now lift thyself; or, if thou prefer it, these men will carry thee; the trouble would not be grudged, since thou and I are of one mind.

Ph. Thanks, my son,—and help me to rise, as thou sayest:—but do not trouble these men, that they may not suffer from the noisome smell before the time. It will be trial enough for them to live on board with me.

Ne. So be it.—Now stand up, and take hold of me thyself.

Ph. Fear not, the old habit will help me to my feet.

Ne. Alack! What am I to do next?

PH. What is the matter, my son? Whither strays thy speech?

NE. I know not how I should turn my faltering words.

PH. Faltering? Wherefore? Say not so, my son.

NE. Indeed, perplexity has now brought me to that pass.

PH. It cannot be that the offence of my disease hath changed thy purpose of receiving me in thy ship?

NE. All is offence when a man hath forsaken his true nature, and is doing what doth not befit him.

PH. Nay, thou, at least, art not departing from thy sire's example in word or deed, by helping one who deserves it.

NE. I shall be found base; this is the thought that torments me.

PH. Not in thy present deeds; but the presage of thy words disquiets me.

NE. O Zeus, what shall I do? Must I be found twice a villain,—by disloyal silence, as well as by shameful speech?

PH. If my judgment errs not, yon man means to betray me, and forsake me, and go his way!

NE. Forsake thee—no; but take thee, perchance, on a bitter voyage—that is the pain that haunts me.

PH. What meanest thou, my son? I understand not.

NE. I will tell thee all. Thou must sail to Troy, to the Achaeans and the host of the Atreidae.

PH. Oh, what hast thou said? NE. Lament not, till thou learn—

PH. Learn what? What would'st thou do to me?

NE. Save thee, first, from this misery,—then go and ravage Troy's plains with thee.

PH. And this is indeed thy purpose? NE. A stern necessity ordains it; be not wroth to hear it.

PH. I am lost, hapless one,—betrayed! What hast thou done unto me, stranger? Restore my bow at once!

NE. Nay, I cannot: duty and policy alike constrain me to obey my chiefs.

PH. Thou fire, thou utter monster, thou hateful masterpiece of subtle villainy,—how hast thou dealt with me, how hast thou deceived me! And thou art not ashamed to look upon me, thou wretch,—the suppliant who turned to thee for pity? In taking my bow, thou hast despoiled me of my life. Restore it, I beseech thee,—restore it, I implore thee, my son! By the gods of thy fathers, do not rob me of my life! Ah me! No—he speaks to me no more; he looks away,—he will not give it up!

O ye creeks and headlands, O ye wild creatures of the hills with whom I dwell, O ye steep cliffs! to you—for to whom else can I speak?—to you, my wonted listeners, I bewail my treatment by the son of Achilles: he swore to convey me home,—to Troy he carries me: he clinched his word with the pledge of his right hand,—yet hath he taken my bow,—the sacred bow, once borne by Heracles son of Zeus,—and keeps it, and would fain show it to the Argives as his own.

He drags me away, as if he had captured a strong man,—and sees not that he is slaying a corpse, the shadow of a vapour, a mere phantom. In my strength he would not have taken me,—no, nor as I am, save by guile. But now I have been tricked, unhappy that I am. What shall I do? Nay, give it back,—return, even now, to thy true self! What sayest thou? Silent? Woe is me, I am lost!

Ah, thou cave with twofold entrance, familiar to mine eyes, once more must I return to thee,—but disarmed, and without the means to live. Yes, in yon chamber my lonely life shall fade away; no winged bird, no beast that roams the hills shall I slay with yonder bow; rather I myself, wretched one, shall make a feast for those who fed me, and become a prey to those on whom I preyed; alas, I shall render my life-blood for the blood which I have shed,—the victim of a man who seemed innocent of evil! Perish!—no, not yet, till I see if thou wilt still change thy purpose;—if thou wilt not, mayest thou die accurs'd!

CH. What shall we do? It now rests with thee, O prince, whether we sail, or hearken to yon man's prayer.

NE. a strange pity for him hath smitten my heart,—and not now for the first time, but long ago.

PH. Show mercy, my son, for the love of the gods, and do not give men cause to reproach thee for having ensnared me.

NE. Ah me, what shall I do? Would I had never left Scyros!—so grievous is my plight.

PH. Thou art no villain; but thou seemest to have come hither as one schooled by villains to a base part. Now leave that part to others, whom it befits, and sail hence,—when thou hast given me. back mine arms.

NE. What shall we do, friends? Odysseus (*appearing suddenly from behind the cave*). Wretch, what art thou doing? Back with thee—and give up this bow to me!

PH. Ah, who is this? Do I hear Odysseus?

OD. Odysseus, be sure of it—me, whom thou beholdest.

PH. Ah me, I am betrayed,—lost! He it was, then, that entrapped me and robbed me of mine arms.

OD. I, surely, and no other I avow it.

PH. Give back my bow,—give it up, my son.

OD. That shall he never do, even if he would. And moreover thou must come along with it, or they will bring thee by force.

PH. What, thou basest and boldest of villains,—are these men to take me by force?

OD. Unless thou come of thy free will.

PH. O Lemnian land, and thou all-conquering flame whose kindler is Hephaestus,—is this indeed to be borne, that yonder man should take me from thy realm by force?

OD. 'Tis Zeus, let me tell thee, Zeus, who rules this land,—Zeus, whose pleasure this is; and I am his servant.

PH. Hateful wretch, what pleas thou canst invent! Sheltering thyself behind gods, thou makest those gods liars.

OD. Nay, true prophets.—Our march must begin.

PH. Never! OD. But I say, Yes. There is no help for it.

PH. Woe is me! Plainly, then, my father begat me to be a slave and no free man.

OD. Nay, but to be the peer of the bravest, with whom thou art destined to take Troy by storm, and raze it to the dust.

PH. No, never,—though I must suffer the worst,—while I have this isle's steep crags beneath me!

OD. What would'st thou do? PH. Throw myself straightway from the rock and shatter this head upon the rock below!

OD. Seize him, both of you! Put it out of his power!

PH. Ah, hands, how ill ye fare, for lack of the bow that ye loved to draw,—yon man's close prisoners! O thou who canst not think one honest or one generous thought, how hast thou once more stolen upon me, how hast thou snared me,—taking this boy for thy screen, a stranger to me,—too good for thy company, but meet for mine,—who had no thought but to perform thy bidding, and who already shows remorse for his own errors and for my wrongs. But thy base soul, ever peering from some ambush, had well trained him,—all unapt and unwilling as he was,—to be cunning in evil.

And now, wretch, thou purposest to bind me hand and foot, and take me from this shore where thou didst fling me forth, friendless, helpless, homeless,—dead among the living!

Alas!

Perdition seize thee! So have I often prayed for thee. But, since the gods grant nothing sweet to me, thou livest and art glad, while life itself is pain to me, steeped in misery as I am,—mocked by thee and by the sons of Atreus, the two chieftains, for whom thou doest this errand. Yet thou sailedst with them only when brought under their yoke by stratagem and constraint; but I—thrice-wretched that I am—joined the fleet of mine own accord, with seven ships, and then was spurned and cast out—by *them*, as thou sayest, or, as they say, by thee.

And now, why would ye take me? why carry me with you? for what purpose? I am nought; for you, I have long been dead. Wretch abhorred of heaven, how is it that thou no longer findest me lame and noisome? How, if I sail with you, can ye burn sacrifices to the gods, or make drink-offerings any more? That was thy pretext for casting me forth.

Miserably may ye perish!—and perish ye shall, for the wrong that ye have wrought against me, if the gods regard justice. But I know that they regard it; for ye would never have come on this voyage in quest of one so wretched, unless some heaven-sent yearning for me had goaded you on.

O, my fatherland, and ye watchful gods, bring your vengeance, bring your vengeance on them all,—at last though late,—if in my lot ye see aught to pity! Yes, a piteous life is mine; but, if I saw those men overthrown, I could dream that I was delivered from my plague.

CH. Bitter with his soul's bitterness are the stranger's words, Odysseus; he bends not before his woes.

OD. I could answer him at length, if leisure served; but now I can say one thing only. Such as the time needs, such am I. Where the question is of just men and good, thou wilt find no man more scrupulous. Victory, however, is my aim in every field,—save with regard to thee: to thee, in this case, I will gladly give way.

Yes, release him, lay no finger upon him more,—let him stay here.—Indeed we have no further need of thee, now that these arms are ours; for Teucer is there to serve us, well-skilled in this craft, and I, who deem that I can wield this bow no whit worse than thou, and point it with as true a hand. What need, then, of thee? Pace thy Lemnos, and joy be with thee! We must be going. And perchance thy treasure will bring to me the honour which ought to have been thine own.

PH. Ah, unhappy that I am, what shall I do? Shalt *thou* be seen among the Argives graced with the arms that are mine?

OD. Bandy no more speech with me—I am going.

PH. Son of Achilles, wilt thou, too, speak no more to me, but depart without a word?

OD. (*to* NE.). Come on! Do not look at him, generous though thou art, lest thou mar our fortune.

PH. (*to* Chorus). Will ye also, friends, indeed leave me thus desolate, and show no pity?

CH. This youth is our commander; whatsoever he saith to thee, that answer is ours also.

NE. (*to* Chorus). I shall be told by my chief that I am too soft-hearted; yet tarry ye here, if yon man will have it so, until the sailors have made all ready on board, and we have offered our prayers to the gods. Meanwhile, perhaps, he may come to a better mind concerning us.—So we two will be going: and ye, when we call you, are to set forth with speed.

[*Exeunt* Odysseus *and* Neoptolemus.

PH. Thou hollow of the caverned rock, now hot, now icy cold,—so, then, it was my hapless destiny never to leave thee! No, thou art to witness my death also. Woe, woe is me! Ah, thou sad dwelling, so long haunted by the pain of my presence, what shall be my daily portion henceforth? Where and whence, wretched that I am, shall I find a hope of sustenance? Above my head, the timorous doves will go on their way through the shrill breeze; for I can arrest their flight no more.

46

CH. 'Tis thou, 'tis thou thyself, ill-fated man, that hast so decreed; this fortune to which thou art captive comes not from without, or from a stronger hand: for, when it was in thy power to show wisdom, thy choice was to reject the better fate, and to accept the worse.

PH. Ah, hapless, hapless then that I am, and broken by suffering; who henceforth must dwell here in my misery, with no man for companion in the days to come, and waste away,—woe, woe, is me,—no longer bringing food to my home, no longer gaining it with the winged weapons held in my strong hands.

But the unsuspected deceits of a treacherous soul beguiled me. Would that I might see him, the contriver of this plot, doomed to my pangs, and for as long a time!

CH. Fate, heaven-appointed fate hath come upon thee in this,—not any treachery to which my hand was lent. Point not at me thy dread and baneful curse! Fain indeed am I that thou shouldest not reject my friendship.

PH. Ah me, ah me! And sitting, I ween, on the marge of the white waves, he mocks me, brandishing the weapon that sustained my hapless life, the weapon which no other living man had borne! Ah, thou well-loved bow, ah, thou that hast been torn from loving hands, surely, if thou canst feel, thou seest with pity that the comrade of Heracles is now to use thee nevermore! Thou hast found a new and wily master; by him art thou wielded; foul deceits thou seest, and the face of that abhorred foe by whom countless mischiefs, springing from vile arts, have been contrived against me,—be thou, O Zeus, my witness!

CH. It is the part of a man ever to assert the right; but, when he hath done so, to refrain from stinging with rancorous taunts. Odysseus was but the envoy of the host, and, at their mandate, achieved a public benefit for his friends.

PH. Ah, my winged prey, and ye tribes of bright-eyed beasts that this place holds in its upland pastures, start no more in flight from your lairs; for I bear not in my hands those shafts which were my strength of old,—ah, wretched that I now am! Nay, roam at large,—the place hath now no more terrors for you,—no more! Now is the moment to take blood for blood,—to glut yourselves at will on my discoloured flesh! Soon shall I pass out of life; for whence shall I find the means to live? Who can feed thus on the winds, when he no longer commands aught that life-giving earth supplies?

CH. For the love of the gods, if thou hast any regard for a friend who draws near to thee in all kindness, approach him ! Nay, consider, consider well, — it is in thine own power to escape from this plague. Cruel is it to him on whom it feeds ; and time cannot teach patience under the countless woes that dwell with it.

PH. Again, again, thou hast recalled the old pain to my thoughts,—kindest though thou art of all who have visited this shore! Why hast thou afflicted me? What hast thou done unto me!

CH. How meanest thou? PH. If it was thy hope to take me to that Trojan land which I abhor.

CH. Nay, so I deem it best. Ph Leave me, then—begone!

CH. Welcome is thy word, right welcome,—I am not loth to obey.—Come, let us be going, each to his place in the ship! [*They begin to move away.*

PH. By the Zeus who hears men's curses, depart not, I implore you! CH. Be calm.

PH. Friends, in the gods' name, stay! CH. Why dost thou call?

PH. Alas, alas! My doom, my doom! Hapless, I am undone! O foot, foot, what shall I do with thee, wretched that I am, in the days to come?—O friends, return!

CH. What would'st thou have us do, different from the purport of thy former bidding?

PH. 'Tis no just cause for anger if one who is distraught with stormy pain speaks frantic words.

CH. Come, then, unhappy man, as we exhort thee.

PH. Never, never,—of that be assured—no, though the lord of the fiery lightning threaten to wrap me in the blaze of his thunderbolts! Perish Ilium, and the men before its walls, who had the heart to spurn me from them, thus crippled! But oh, my friends, grant me one boon!

CH. What would'st thou ask?

Pн. A sword, if ye can find one, or an axe, or any weapon,—oh, bring it to me!

Cн. What rash deed would'st thou do?

Pн. Mangle this body utterly,—hew limb from limb with mine own hand! Death, death is my thought now—

Cн. What means this? Pн. I would seek my sire—

Cн. In what land? Pн. In the realm of the dead; he is in the sunlight no more. Ah, my home, city of my fathers! Would I might behold thee,—misguided, indeed, that I was, who left thy sacred stream, and went forth to help the Danai, mine enemies!—Undone—undone!

Cн. Long since should I have left thee, and should now have been near my ship, had I not seen Odysseus approaching, and the son of Achilles, too, coming hither to us.

Enter Neoptolemus, *followed by* Odysseus.

Oд. Wilt thou not tell me on what errand thou art returning in such hot haste?

Nе. To undo the fault that I committed before.

Oд. A strange saying; and what was the fault?

Nе. When, obeying thee and all the host—

Oд. What deed didst thou, that became thee not?

Nе. When I ensnared a man with base fraud and guile.

Oд. Whom? Alas!—canst thou be planning some rash act?

Nе. Rash,—no: but to the son of Poeas—

Oд. What wilt thou do? A strange fear comes over me...

50

NE. —from whom I took this bow, to him again—

OD. Zeus! what would'st thou say? Thou wilt not give it back?

NE. Yea, I have gotten it basely and without right.

OD. In the name of the gods, sayest thou this to mock me?

NE. If it be mockery to speak the truth.

OD. What meanest thou, son of Achilles? What hast thou said?

NE. Must I repeat the same words twice and thrice?

OD. I should have wished not to hear them at all.

NE. Rest assured that I have nothing more to say.

OD. There is a power, I tell thee, that shall prevent thy deed.

NE. What meanest thou? Who is to hinder me in this?

OD. The whole host of the Achaeans,—and I for one.

NE. Wise though thou be, thy words are void of wisdom.

OD. Thy speech is not wise, nor yet thy purpose.

NE. But if just, that is better than wise.

OD. And how is it just, to give up what thou hast won by my counsels? NE. My fault hath been shameful, and I must seek to retrieve it.

OD. Hast thou no fear of the Achaean host, in doing this?

NE. With justice on my side, I do not fear thy terrors.

[OD. But I will compel thee.]

NE. Nay, not even to thy force do I yield obedience.

OD. Then we shall fight, not with the Trojans, but with thee.

NE. Come, then, what must. OD. Seest thou my right hand on my sword-hilt? NE. Nay, thou shalt see me doing the same, and that promptly.

OD. Well, I will take no more heed of thee; but I will go and tell this to all the host, and by them thou shalt be punished.

NE. Thou hast come to thy senses; and if thou art thus prudent henceforth, perchance thou mayest keep clear of trouble.

[*Exit* Odysseus.

But thou, O son of Poeas, Philoctetes, come forth, leave the shelter of thy rocky home!

PH. (*within*). What means this noise of voices once more rising beside my cave?

Why do you call me forth? What would ye have of me, sirs?

[*He appears at the mouth of the cave, and sees* Neoptolemus.

Ah me! this bodes no good. Can ye have come as heralds of new woes for me, to crown the old?

NE. Fear not, but hearken to the words that I bring.

Ph. I am afraid. Fair words brought me evil fortune once before, when I believed thy promises.

Ne. Is there no room, then, for repentance?

Ph. Even such wast thou in speech, when seeking to steal my bow,—a trusty friend, with treason in his heart.

Ne. But not so now;—and I fain would learn whether thy resolve is to abide here and endure, or to sail with us.

Ph. Stop, speak no more! All that thou canst say will be said in vain.

Ne. Thou art resolved? Ph. More firmly, believe me, than speech can tell.

Ne. Well, I could have wished that thou hadst listened to my words; but if I speak not in season, I have done. Ph. Aye, thou wilt say all in vain.

Never canst thou win the amity of my soul, thou who hast taken the stay of my life by fraud, and robbed me of it,—and then hast come here to give me counsel—thou most hateful offspring of a noble sire! Perdition seize you all, the Atreidae first, and next the son of Laertes, and thee! Ne. Utter no more curses; but receive these weapons from my hand.

Ph. What sayest thou? Am I being tricked a second time?

Ne. No, I swear it by the pure majesty of Zeus most high!

Ph. O welcome words,—if thy words be true!

Ne. The deed shall soon prove the word:—come, stretch

forth thy right hand, and be master of thy bow!

[*As he hands the bow and arrows to* Philoctetes,
Odysseus *suddenly appears.*

OD. But I forbid it—be the gods my witnesses—in the name of the Atreidae and all the host!

PH. My son, whose voice was that? Did I hear Odysseus?
OD. Be sure of it,—and thou seest him at thy side,—who will carry thee to the plains of Troy perforce, whether the son of Achilles will or no.

PH. But to thy cost, if this arrow fly straight.

[*Bends his bow.*

NE. (*seizing his arm*). Ah, for the gods' love, forbear—launch not thy shaft!

PH. Unhand me, in Heaven's name, dear youth!

NE. I will not. PH. Alas! why hast thou disappointed me of slaying my hated enemy with my bow!

NE. Nay, it suits not with my honour, nor with thine.

[*Exit* Odysseus.

PH. Well, thou mayest be sure of one thing,—that the chiefs of the host, the lying heralds of the Greeks, though brave with words, are cowards in fight.

NE. Good; the bow is thine; and thou hast no cause of anger or complaint against me.

PH. I grant it; and thou hast shown the race, my son, from which thou springest,—no child, thou, of Sisyphus, but of Achilles, whose fame was fairest when he was with the living, as it is now among the dead.

NE. Sweet to me is thy praise of my sire, and of myself; but hear the boon that I am fain to win from thee. Men must needs bear the fortunes given by the gods; but when they cling to self-inflicted miseries, as thou dost, no one can justly excuse or pity them. Thou hast become intractable; thou canst tolerate no counsellor; and if one advise thee, speaking with good will, thou hatest him, deeming him a foe who wishes thee ill. Yet I will speak, calling Zeus to witness, who hears men's oaths; and do thou mark these words, and write them in thy heart.

Thou sufferest this sore plague by a heaven-sent doom, because thou didst draw near to Chrysè's watcher, the serpent, secret warder of her home, that guards her roofless sanctuary. And know that relief from this grievous sickness can never be thy portion, so long as the sun still rises in the east and sets in the west, until thou come, of thine own free will, to the plains of Troy, where thou shalt meet with the sons of Asclepius, our comrades, and shalt be eased of this malady; and, with this bow's aid and mine, shalt achieve the capture of the Ilian towers.

I will tell thee how I know that these things are so ordained. We have a Trojan prisoner, Helenus, foremost among seers; who saith plainly that all this must come to pass; and further, that this present summer must see the utter overthrow of Troy: or else he is willing that his life be forfeit, if this his word prove false.

Now, therefore, that thou knowest this, yield with a good grace; 'tis a glorious heightening of thy gain, to be singled out as bravest of the Greeks,—first, to come into healing hands,—then to take the Troy of many tears, and so to win a matchless renown.

PH. O hateful life, why, why dost thou keep me in the light of day, instead of suffering me to seek the world of the dead? Ah me, what shall I do? How can I be deaf to this man's words, who hath counselled me with kindly purpose? But shall I yield, then? How, after doing that, shall I come into men's sight, wretched that I am? Who will speak to me? Ye eyes that have beheld all my wrongs, how could ye endure to see me consorting with the sons of Atreus, who wrought my ruin, or with the accursed son of Laertes?

It is not the resentment for the past that stings me,—I seem to foresee what I am doomed to suffer from these men in the future; for, when the mind hath once become a parent of evil, it teaches men to be evil thenceforth. And in thee, too, this conduct moves my wonder. It behoved thee never to revisit Troy thyself, and to hinder me from going thither; seeing that those men have done thee outrage, by wresting from thee the honours of thy sire; [they, who in their award of thy father's arms, adjudged the hapless Ajax inferior to Odysseus:]—after that, wilt thou go to fight at their side,—and wouldest thou constrain me to do likewise?

Nay, do not so, my son; but rather, as thou hast sworn to me, convey me home; and, abiding in Scyros thyself, leave those evil men to their evil doom. So shalt thou win double thanks from me, as from my sire, and shalt not seem, through helping bad men, to be like them in thy nature.

NE. There is reason in what thou sayest; nevertheless, I would have thee put thy trust in the gods and in my words, and sail forth from this land with me, thy friend.

PH. What! to the plains of Troy, and to the abhorred son of Atreus,—with this wretched foot?

NE. Nay, but to those who will free thee and thine ulcered limb from pain, and will heal thy sickness.

PH. Thou giver of dire counsel, what canst thou mean?

NE. What I see is fraught with the best issue for us both.

PH. Hast thou no shame that the gods should hear those words?

NE. Why should a man be ashamed of benefiting his friends?

PH. Is this benefit to the Atreidae, or for me?

NE. For thee, I ween: I am thy friend, and speak in friendship.

PH. How so, when thou would'st give me up to my foes?

NE. Prithee, learn to be less defiant in misfortune.

PH. Thou wilt ruin me, I know thou wilt, with these words.

NE. *I* will not; but I say that thou dost not understand.

PH. Do I not know that the Atreidae cast me out?

NE. They cast thee out, but look if they will not restore thee to welfare.

PH. Never,—if I must first consent to visit Troy.

NE. What am I to do, then, if my pleading cannot win thee to aught that I urge? The easiest course for me is that I should cease from speech, and that thou shouldest live, even as now, without deliverance.

PH. Let me bear the sufferings that are my portion; but the promise which thou madest to me, with hand laid in mine,—to bring me home,—that promise do thou fulfil, my son; and tarry not, nor speak any more of Troy; for the measure of my lamentation is full.

NE. If thou wilt, let us be going. PH. O generous word!

NE. Now plant thy steps firmly. PH. To the utmost of my strength.

NE. But how shall I escape blame from the Achaeans? PH. Heed it not.

NE. What if they ravage my country? PH. I will be there—

NE. And what help wilt thou render? PH. With the shafts of Heracles—

NE. What is thy meaning?—PH.—I will keep them afar.

NE. Take thy farewell of this land, and set forth.

HERACLES *APPEARS ABOVE THEM.*

HE. Nay, not yet, till thou hast hearkened unto my words, son of Poeas: know that the voice of Heracles soundeth in thine ears, and thou lookest upon his face.

For thy sake have I come from the heavenly seats, to show thee the purposes of Zeus, and to stay the journey whereon thou art departing; give thou heed unto my counsel.

First I would tell thee of mine own fortunes,—how, after enduring many labours to the end, I have won deathless glory, as thou behold est. And for thee, be sure, the destiny is ordained that through these thy sufferings thou shouldest glorify thy life.

Thou shalt go with yon man to the Trojan city, where, first, thou shalt be healed of thy sore malady; then, chosen out as foremost in prowess of the host, with my bow shalt thou slay Paris, the author of these ills; thou shalt sack Troy; the prize of valour shall be given to thee by our warriors; and thou shalt carry the spoils to thy home, for the joy of Poeas thy sire, even to thine own Oetaean heights. And whatsoever spoils thou receivest from that host, thence take a thank-offering for my bow unto my pyre.

(And these my counsels are for thee also, son of Achilles; for thou canst not subdue the Trojan realm without his help, nor he without thine: ye are as lions twain that roam together; each of you guards the other's life.)

For the healing of thy sickness, I will send Asclepius to Troy; since it is doomed to fall a second time before mine arrows. But of this be mindful, when ye lay waste the land,—that ye show reverence towards the gods. All things else are of less account in the sight of our father Zeus; for piety dies not with men; in their life and in their death, it is immortal.

PH. Ah, thou whose accents I had yearned to hear, thou whose form is seen after many days, I will not disobey thy words!

NE. I, too, consent.

HE. Tarry not long, then, ere ye act; for occasion urges, and the fair wind yonder at the stern.

PH. Come, then, let me greet this land, as I depart. Farewell, thou chamber that hast shared my watches, farewell, ye nymphs of stream and meadow, and thou, deep voice of the sea-lashed cape,—where, in the cavern's inmost recess, my head was often wetted by the south-wind's blasts, and where oft the Hermaean mount sent an echo to my mournful cries, in the tempest of my sorrow!

But now, O ye springs, and thou Lycian fount, I am leaving you,—leaving you at last,—I, who had never attained to such a hope!

Farewell, thou sea-girt Lemnos; and speed me with fair course, for my contentment, to that haven whither I am borne by mighty fate, and by the counsel of friends, and by the all-subduing god who hath brought these things to fulfilment.

Cн. Now let us all set forth together, when we have made our prayer to the Nymphs of the sea, that they come to us for the prospering of our return.

A NOTE ON THE HISTORY OF PHILOSOPHY

T O philosophize is to reflect; to examine things, in thought.

Yet in this is the conception of philosophy not sufficiently defined. Man, as thinking, also employs those practical activities concerned in the adaptation of means to an end; the whole body of sciences also, even those which do not in strict sense belong to philosophy, still lie in the realm of thought. In what, then, is philosophy distinguished from these sciences, e. g. from the science of astronomy, of medicine, or of rights? Certainly not in that it has a different material to work upon. Its material is precisely the same as that of the different empirical sciences. The construction and disposition of the universe, the arrangement and functions of the human body, the doctrines of property, of rights and of the state—all these materials belong as truly to philosophy as to their appropriate sciences. That which is given in the world of experience, that which is real, is the content likewise of philosophy. It is not, therefore, in its material but in its form, in its method, in its mode of knowledge, that philosophy is to be distinguished from the empirical sciences. These latter derive their material directly from experience; they find it at hand and take it up just as they find it. Philosophy, on the other hand, is never satisfied with receiving that which is given simply as it is given, but rather follows it out to its ultimate grounds; it examines every individual thing in reference to a final principle, and considers it as one link in the whole chain of knowledge. In this way philosophy removes from the individual thing given in experience, its immediate, individual, and accidental character; from the sea of empirical individualities, it brings out that which is common to all; from the infinite and orderless mass of contingencies it finds that which is necessary, and throws over all a universal law. In short, philosophy examines the *totality* of experience in the form of an *organic system* in harmony with the laws of thought. From the above it is seen, that philosophy (in the sense we have given it) and the empirical sciences have a reciprocal influence; the latter conditioning the former, while they at the same time are conditioned by it. We shall, therefore, in the history of the world, no more find an absolute and complete philosophy, than a complete empirical science (*Empirik*). Rather is philosophy found only in the form of the different philosophical systems, which have successively appeared in the course of history, advancing hand in hand with the progress of the empirical sciences and the universal, social, and civil culture, and showing in their advance the different steps in the development and improvement of human science. The history of philosophy has, for its object, to represent the content, the succession, and the inner connection of these philosophical systems.

The relation of these different systems to each other is thus already intimated. The historical and collective life of the race is bound together by the idea of a spiritual and intellectual progress, and manifests a regular order of advancing, though not always continuous, stages of development. In this, the fact harmonizes with what we should expect from antecedent probabilities. Since, therefore, every philosophical system is only the philosophical expression of the collective life of its time, it follows that these different systems which have appeared in history will disclose one organic movement and form together one rational and internally connected (*gegliedertes*) system. In all their developments, we shall find one constant order, grounded in the striving of the spirit ever to raise itself to a higher point of consciousness and knowledge, and to recognize the whole spiritual and natural universe, more and more, as its outward being, as its reality, as the mirror of itself.

Hegel was the first to utter these thoughts and to consider the history of philosophy as a united process, but this view, which is, in its principle, true, he has applied in a way which would destroy the freedom of human actions, and remove the very conception of contingency, *i. e.* that any thing should be contrary to reason. Hegel's view is, that the succession of the systems of philosophy which have appeared in history, corresponds to the succession of logical categories in a system of logic. According to him, if, from the fundamental conceptions of these different philosophical systems, we remove that which pertains to their outward form or particular application, &c., so do we find the different steps of the logical conceptions (*e. g.* being, becoming, existence, being *per se* (*fürsichseyn*) quantity, &c.). And on the other hand, if we take up the logical process by itself, we find also in it the actual historical process.

This opinion, however, can be sustained neither in its principle nor in its historical application. It is defective in its principle, because in history freedom and necessity inter-penetrate, and, therefore, while we find, if we consider it in its general aspects, a rational connection running through the whole, we also see, if we look solely at its individual parts, only a play of numberless contingencies, just as the kingdom of nature, taken as a whole, reveals a rational plan in its successions, but viewed only in its parts, mocks at every attempt to reduce them to a preconceived plan. In history we have to do with free subjectivities, with indi-viduals capable of originating actions, and have, therefore, a factor which does not admit of a previous calculation. For however accurately we may estimate the controlling conditions which may attach to an individual, from the general circumstances in which he may be placed, his age, his associations, his nationality, &c., a free will can never be calculated like a mathematical problem. History is no example for a strict arithmetical calculation. The history of philosophy, therefore, cannot admit of an apriori construc-tion; the actual occurrences should not be joined together as illustrative of a preconceived plan; but the facts, so far as they can be admitted, after a critical sifting, should be received as such, and their rational connection be analytically determined. The speculative idea can only supply the law for the arrangement and scientific connection of that which may be historically furnished.

A more comprehensive view, which contradicts the above-given Hegelian notion, is the following. The actual historical development is, very generally, different from the theoretical. Historically *e. g.* the State arose as a means of protection against robbers, while theoretically it is derived from the idea of rights. So also, even in the actual history of philosophy, while the logical (theoretical) process is an ascent from the abstract to the concrete, yet does the historical development of philosophy, quite generally, descend from the concrete to the abstract, from intuition to thought, and separates the abstract from the concrete in those general forms of culture and those religious and social circumstances, in which the philosophizing subject is placed. A *system* of philosophy proceeds synthetically, while the *history* of philosophy, *i. e.* the history of the thinking process proceeds analytically. We might, therefore, with great propriety, adopt directly the reverse of the Hegelian position, and say that what in reality is the first, is for us, in fact, the last. This is illustrated in the Ionic philosophy. It began not with being as an abstract conception, but with the most concrete, and most apparent, *e. g.* with the material conception of water, air, &c. Even if we leave the Ionics and advance to the being of the Eleatics or the becoming of the Heraclitics, we find, that these, instead of being pure thought determinations, are only unpurified conceptions, and materially colored intuitions. Still farther, is the attempt impracticable to refer every philosophy that has appeared in history to some logical category as its central principle, because the most of these philosophies have taken, for their object, the idea, not as an abstract conception, but in its realization as nature and mind, and, therefore, for the most part, have to do, not with logical questions, but with those relating to natural philosophy, psychology and ethics. Hegel should not, therefore, limit his comparison of the historical and systematic process of development simply to logic, but should extend it to the whole system of philosophical science. Granted that the Eleatics, the Heraclitics and the Atomists may have made such a category as the centre of their systems, and we may find thus far the Hegelian logic in harmony with the Hegelian history of philosophy. But if we go farther, how is it? How with Anaxagoras, the Sophists, Socrates, Plato, Aristotle? We cannot, certainly, without violence, press one central principle into the systems of these men, but if we should be able to do it, and could reduce *e. g.* the philosophy of Anaxagoras to the conception of "the end," that of the Sophists to the conception of "the appearance," and the Socratic Philosophy to the conception of "the good,"— yet even then we have the new difficulty that the historical does not correspond to the logical succession of these categories. In fact, Hegel himself has not attempted a complete application of his principle, and indeed gave it up at the very threshold of the Grecian philosophy. To the Eleatics, the Heraclitics and the Atomists, the logical categories of "being," "becoming," and being *per se* may be successively ascribed, and so far, as already remarked, the parallelism extends, but no farther. Not only does Anaxagoras follow with the conception of reason working according to an end, but if we go back before the Eleatics, we find in the very beginning of philosophy a total diversity between the logical and historical order. If Hegel had carried out his principle consistently, he should have thrown away entirely the Ionic philosophy, for matter is no logical category; he should have placed the Pythagoreans after the Eleatics and the Atomists, for in logical order the categories of quantity follow those of quality; in short, he would have been obliged to set aside all chronology. Unless this be done, we must be satisfied with a theoretical reproduction of the course which the thinking spirit has taken in its history, only so far as we can see in the grand stages of history a rational progress of thought; only so far as the philosophical historian, surveying a period of development, actually finds in it a philosophical acquisition,—the acquisition of a new idea: but we must guard ourselves against applying to the transition and intermediate steps, as well as to the whole detail of history, the postulate of an immanent conformity to law, or an organism in harmony with our own thoughts. History often winds its way like a serpent in lines which appear retrogressive, and philosophy, especially, has not seldom withdrawn herself from a wide and already fruitful field, in order to settle down upon a narrow strip of land, the limits even of which she has sought still more closely to abridge. At one time we find thousands of years expended in fruitless attempts with only a negative result;—at another, a fulness of philosophical ideas are crowded together in the experience of a lifetime. There is here no sway of an immutable and regularly returning law, but history, as the realm of freedom, will first completely manifest itself at the end of time as the work of reason.

Excerpt from *A History of Philosophy in Epitome* by Albert Schwegler.

Made in United States
North Haven, CT
05 August 2022

22331565R00046